I am a drop of water living on a blue planet.
Since its birth, I've been on a long, long journey . . .

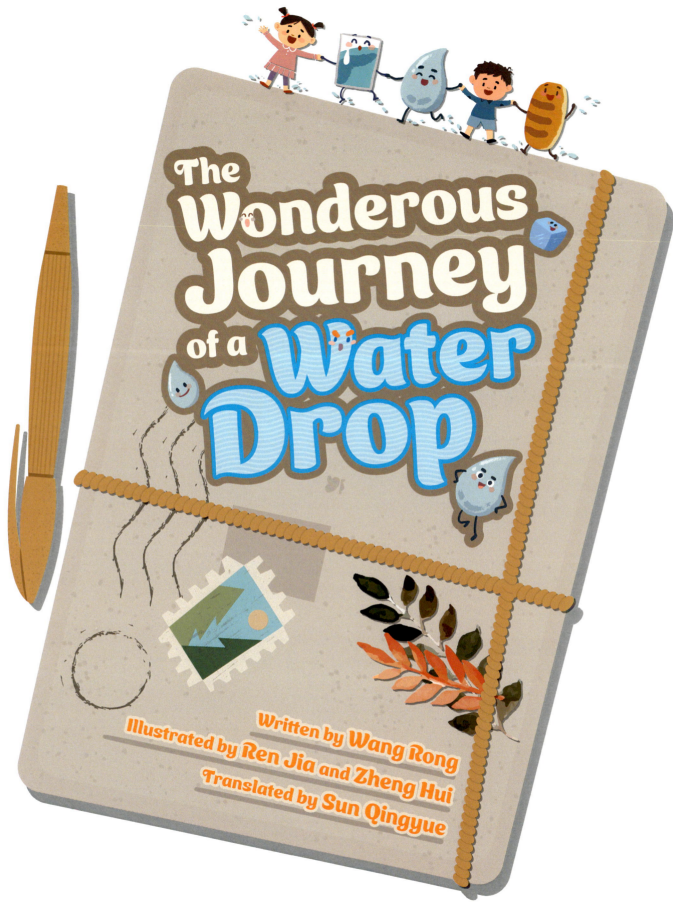

The Wonderous Journey of a Water Drop

Written by Wang Rong
Illustrated by Ren Jia and Zheng Hui
Translated by Sun Qingyue

Books Beyond Boundaries
ROYAL COLLINS

Contents

The Secrets of the Blue Planet 4

The Sea Is a Blue Cradle 6

Friends from the Deep Ocean 8

Welcome to the Earth's Botanic Garden 10

Hello! Dinosaur Family 12

Spreading Wings Open or Drilling out of the Ground 14

Footsteps of Humanity 16

Stories Flowing by the Riverbank 18

When the River Gets Angry   20

The Ingenious Chinese   22

Water Drop's New Game   24

Along the Sea to Afar   26

World-Changing Machines   28

Cities Bathed in Waterlight   30

Scary and Dangerous Things   32

Saving a Water Drop   34

The Secrets of the Blue Planet

A smoking volcano told me that this blue planet is called Earth. It was born in a Big Bang in the universe, and I heard that the newly born Earth didn't look like this now.

Stories of the Solar Family

After the Big Bang, tons of stars popped out all over the universe, and the Sun is one of them. Nearby the Sun, there floated rocks and dust. They did collide but also embraced each other from time to time. Soon, eight weird planets were born. They revolve around the Sun, forming the solar system with their other celestial friends.

There is iron in the soil on Mars. So, it's reddish.

The Sun is like a giant fireball. Its center is even hotter than 15,000,000°C. Inside, something called nuclear fusion is happening all the time—a bunch of tiny, invisible fireworks going off nonstop.

Earth's gravity holds tight onto the air. Then, it gets the atmosphere.

Mercury is the smallest member of the solar family, which stays closest to the Sun. One of its sides is scorching hot, while the other is freezing cold.

Venus is covered in fluffy blankets of clouds and mysterious mist.

Uranus is blue because its atmosphere is filled with a lot of methane.

The icy Neptune lives the farthest.

Jupiter is the largest and heaviest member of the family, but it is almost made of gas. Whirling storms in its atmosphere painted the clouds colorful, different from all the others.

Saturn wears a spectacular ring. Just like Jupiter, it is also a star of gas.

The Earth as It Was When It Was Born

The newborn Earth was a hot furnace, with volcanoes spewing smoke and lava everywhere and meteors endlessly falling from the sky.

Later, meteors visited the Earth less often, and the Earth's surface slowly lowered its temperature.

The lava from the volcano began to cool and harden, turning into a bumpy cratered crust, which became the Earth's very first land.

The Sea Is a Blue Cradle

A Sea Fell from the Sky

Smoke from the volcanoes drifted to the sky without resting. These gases wrapped around the Earth, creating a dense atmosphere and wandering clouds.

The Earliest Life

After hundreds of millions of years of waiting, the substances in the ocean gave birth to the earliest life, although it was just a simple cell.

Cyanobacteria, through photosynthesis, absorbed carbon dioxide and released oxygen, becoming the earliest oxygen producers on Earth. Through their relentless efforts, these gases filled the atmosphere, giving life to more complex species …

One of the earliest single-celled organisms is cyanobacteria.

After the Earth became cooler, when gusts of wind blew into the sky, these clouds would fall to the ground as rain.

When the weather got too hot, some of the raindrops chose to evaporate and float back up to the clouds.

While the others traveled along the lands, finally joining each other to form the earliest sea.

Chemical substances swam in the sea. There were hydrogen, nitrogen, carbon, oxygen, sulfur, and so on. Under the beams of sunlight and the rumbles of thunder, they magically began to transform…

Usually, when the temperature exceeds 100°C, water boils and turns into steam.

When the temperature is below 0°C, water freezes into ice.

At temperatures between 0°C and 100°C, water is liquid.

Different temperatures give me different transformation abilities!

Friends from the Deep Ocean

About 500 million years ago, I met a variety of strange friends in the deep blue sea. Some were like bugs bigger than umbrellas, some waved their tentacles in the water like birds flapping their wings, and some even grew "equipment" to leave the ocean.

Trilobites That Took Over the World

On the early seabed, creatures called trilobites crawled slowly. They were highly adaptable, capable of swimming and floating, and when faced with fearsome enemies, they could curl up with their spiked armor for defense. Over their 300 million years on Earth, they evolved into many different species. The longest trilobites could reach over 90 centimeters, while the shortest were only about one millimeter long.

Two noticeable ridges ran down their backs, making their bodies look like they were split into three sections. That's how the trilobite got its name.

Kunming Fish Standing Upright

In addition to trilobites growing their tribes, the fish in the sea were not to be outdone. They developed a notochord, allowing their bodies to perform more complex movements. Kunming fish, with a body length of less than three centimeters and a height of less than six millimeters, were small but were among the earliest animals in the ocean to develop a notochord.

The notochord can support a soft body, but it is not a hard bone; it is more like elastic cartilage. Later, many animals gave up their less robust notochords and developed more durable spines.

Nautilus That Escaped Doomsday

The nautilus is a famous "living fossil." With their parrot-beak-shaped spiral shells, they have survived five mass extinctions to the present day. With their large bodies and bad temper, the nautilus quickly overtook the trilobites as the ocean's dominant species. They often secrete sticky liquid from their tentacles and ambush rocks on the seafloor, waiting for the moon to rise before they begin their ferocious hunt.

Entelognathus the Meat Lover

As more life filled the ocean, it became an increasingly dangerous environment. To survive, some creatures have evolved jawbones that allow them to open and close their mouths for hunting. The jawbones of Entelognathus were so well designed that they became models that other animals strived to emulate.

About 400 million years ago, the Earth became so hot that there was less and less water in the oceans and lakes through evaporation. The shrinking ocean was full of predators with gap-open mouths, so some sea creatures who wanted to live were ready to move on land...

The Secrets of Amphibians

Amphibians undergo metamorphosis. There is a significant difference in appearance and lifestyle between their juvenile and adult stages. Ichthyostega lived in the water when they were young and breathed through their gills, but as adults, they often stayed on land and breathed through their lungs.

Their neck joints allowed their heads to move more freely, helping them to better spot prey and danger.

Their eyelids helped keep their eyes moist and protect them from the wind and sand on land.

Their exposed skin secreted a sticky fluid that helped them breathe.

Their limbs that evolved from fish fins allowed them to move easily and crawl on land.

The Most Successful Lander and the Most Primitive Amphibian, Ichthyostega

Welcome to the Earth's Botanic Garden

In fact, by the time ocean-dwelling animals were preparing to venture onto land, the plants of the sea had already begun their journey with me. We searched for a place to settle on the scorching, cracked earth, tracked the sun's position under the cloudy sky, waded through rivers, crossed canyons, and climbed mountains. In the unknown seasons of an endless journey, these plants displayed dazzling forms and transformations...

Bryophyte

Around 480 million years ago, algae "crawled" from the sea to land. The dry, water-scarce earth hindered their footsteps.

Some bent down their bodies, allowing their leaves to lie flat on the ground to absorb water from the soil.

Some threw away bulky leaves and shrank them into small fluff to lay on the ground to reduce water loss.

These changes made them terrestrial bryophytes.

Sun-Loving Ferns

Having solved the problem of water scarcity, some plants began to yearn for the warmth of sunlight. They developed vascular tissues resembling skeletal structures to support their bodies, growing desperately toward the sky to absorb more sunlight.

The vascular tube is like a straw, sucking water and nutrients from the ground and transporting them to various body parts. Those who concentrated on growing upward and forgetting to develop leaves became the land's early vascular plants. They are considered the ancestors of higher plants on Earth.

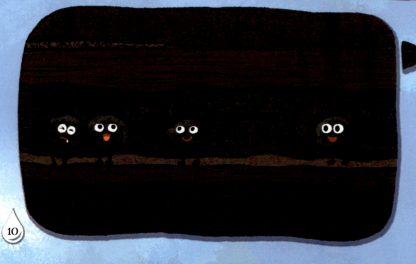

Later, some ferns grew taller and developed lush leaves, forming the first primeval forests on land. However, over 200 million years ago, these towering plants perished and were deeply buried underground. Millions of years later, they transformed into coal, waiting to be discovered.

The Battle between Spores and Seeds

Mosses and ferns both reproduce through spores. However, spores are delicate cells that require a warm, moist environment to thrive and grow properly.

As a result, some plants produce seeds that are protected by seed coats and can reproduce in an undemanding environment. Seeds are much larger than spores and can store more nutrients. Plants that produce seeds quickly spread across the land and can be classified into naked-seed plants called gymnosperms and flowering plants called angiosperms.

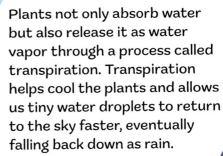

Plants not only absorb water but also release it as water vapor through a process called transpiration. Transpiration helps cool the plants and allows us tiny water droplets to return to the sky faster, eventually falling back down as rain.

Flowering Angiosperms That Grow Fruits

Angiosperm seeds are encased in thick fruit skins, which can be seen all over the Earth. They come in a wide variety of forms and are the most diverse family of plants, ranging from towering trees to inconspicuous grasses.

Non-flowering Gymnosperms That Rarely Grow Fruit

The seeds of gymnosperms are exposed without the protection of fruit skins. Nevertheless, it still allows them to live everywhere. For example, conifer and ginkgo are common gymnosperms.

Hello! Dinosaur Family

Dinosaurs were the most memorable friends I've ever met on my long journey. Some were bigger than mountains, others were skinny but could run faster than lightning. It is said that their ancestors were reptiles, which evolved from amphibians more than 300 million years ago.

Secrets of Reptiles

Covered in scales or thick keratin, reptiles protect their bodies and prevent water loss.

Eoraptor

They were one of the earliest and most primitive dinosaurs discovered so far.

They breathe using their lungs and do not chew their food; instead, they swallow it whole.

Ectothermic animals, also known as cold-blooded animals, mostly live in warm climates. They hibernate in the cold winter and sometimes in the hot summer.

Reptiles crawl on all fours. However, dinosaurs were unique; their limbs were positioned directly underneath their bodies rather than on the sides like others. This allowed the dinosaurs to stand up, making it easier for them to walk and run. Some dinosaurs even moved only on their hind legs, using their forelimbs to catch prey.

Hear More Sounds

Middle ears developed by reptiles soon became the model for many vertebrates to copy. Thanks to this, many animals started to have much better hearing.

Ears evolved slowly from the gill arches of fish.

The gill arches first evolved into the hyoid bone.

The hyoid bone separated from the jawbone and evolved into the ear ossicles.

Eudimorphodon
Their tail had a diamond-shaped vane used for controlling direction during flight.

Most dinosaurs I know lived on land, but some could fly in the sky. Among them were gentle herbivores, meat-loving gluttons, and omnivores that ate everything without being picky.

Sinosauropteryx
They had brown-orange striped feathers and were very good at running.

Triceratops
They used the horns on their heads for fighting and courting. While looking fierce, they were herbivores who loved to eat grass.

Tyrannosaurus Rex
They were the most famous carnivorous dinosaur, extremely fierce with a gigantic body.

Diplodocus
They were dinosaurs with exceptionally long bodies. Its neck could grow to over 7 meters, and its tail could reach up to 13 meters.

Placochelys
They had flippers similar to sea turtles. Their sharp beaks could crush the shells of bottom-dwelling sea creatures.

Spreading Wings Open or Drilling out of the Ground

Traveling on Earth often brings surprises and joy, but it is sometimes met with disaster and sadness. When the Earth became more and more blue, frightening meteors frequently intruded the sky. They slammed into the ground, causing the Earth to tremble with pain, volcanoes to erupt lava in horror, and the sea to stir up giant waves of anger. During these times, I could only escape into the sky, fleeing amid thick smoke and continuing my wandering there. When I finally returned to the ground, many friends had vanished without a trace…

> These birds flying in the sky often make me wonder if they evolved from dinosaurs. Why else would they have so many dinosaur-like features?

Both a Dinosaur and a Bird—Archaeopteryx

Archaeopteryx, which appeared about 145 million years ago, might be one of the oldest birds in the world. It had both bird and dinosaur characteristics, which is often cited as evidence that dinosaurs evolved into birds.

The Five Mass Extinctions

- **Ordovician–Silurian Extinction (about 440 million years ago)**
  Approximately 85% of species went extinct. Jawed vertebrates took this opportunity to expand their populations.

- **Late Devonian Extinction (about 370 million years ago)**
  Approximately 75% of species went extinct. Many animals developed limbs to explore land for survival. The age of amphibians began on Earth.

- **Permian–Triassic Extinction (about 252 million years ago)**
  Approximately 96% of marine species and 70% of terrestrial species went extinct. The nearly emptied Earth awaited the rise of reptiles.

- **Triassic–Jurassic Extinction (about 200 million years ago)**
  About 75% of all living things became extinct, and the oceans became a major disaster zone. After the disaster, the Earth would welcome the dinosaur overlords.

- **Cretaceous–Paleogene Extinction (about 66 million years ago)**
  Approximately 75% of species went extinct. The disappearance of dinosaurs created new opportunities for timid mammals.

The Secrets about Birds

They do not have teeth but instead have hard beaks.

Most birds gain the ability to fly from their streamlined bodies, thin bones, and wings developed from forelimbs.

They reproduce through oviparity. Oviparity means that the fertilized egg grows independently outside the mother's body. Simply put, the baby hatches from an egg.

Bats
They are the only mammals capable of flying in the sky.

Secrets of the Mammals
Most members of the mammal family are covered in fur.
    They have external ears that give them good hearing ability.
    They have multi-functional teeth.
    They breathe with lungs.
    Most of them are viviparous.
    Viviparous means that the fertilized egg grows inside the mother's body. Simply put, the baby is born as a more fullly developed little animal.

Morganucodon
They appeared around 200 million years ago and were a representative of early mammals. Although small and primitive, they might have been the ancestors of most mammals.

Dipodidae
It looks like a miniature kangaroo with exceptional jumping ability, able to leap over a meter high. It still lives on the plains of Africa today.

Juramaia Sinensis
With a long tail and limbs, it moved very quickly, like a little mouse. It might have been the first mammal to have a placenta.

Sabertooth Tiger
With a body size one time larger than that of a lion and a pair of long, sharp teeth, the ferocious saber-toothed tiger was feared by all animals of its time. Unfortunately, it went extinct about ten thousand years ago.

Mammoth
They could live in extremely cold places and were the largest land mammals that ever existed. However, they went extinct over ten thousand years ago.

Pakicetus
They were the oldest known whale species.

Footsteps of Humanity

From Ancient Apes to Homo Sapiens

Around 10 million years ago
With the massive disappearance of forests, the ancient forest apes learned to walk upright.

Around 5.8 million years ago
Ardipithecus, which possessed both ape and hominid characteristics, began to appear.

Around 2.9 million to 3.9 million years ago
Australopithecus afarensis, who gathered plants and fruits, began living on the land.

A Journey inside the Human Body

Humans are the most amazing mammals I have ever seen. To study them, I went on an extraordinary journey.

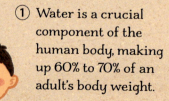

① Water is a crucial component of the human body, making up 60% to 70% of an adult's body weight.

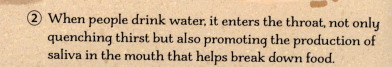

② When people drink water, it enters the throat, not only quenching thirst but also promoting the production of saliva in the mouth that helps break down food.

Around 2.5 million years ago
The skilled Homo habilis appeared; they could make stone tools, hunt small prey, and build simple shelters.

Around 200 thousand to 2 million years ago
Homo erectus, with its perfect upright posture, roamed the land.

Around 10 thousand to 200 thousand years ago
Homo sapiens, much like modern humans, made sophisticated tools and ornaments, and they developed their own culture and pursuit of beauty.

③ Water passes through the digestive tract and moistens the mucous membranes on the nasopharynx and trachea, making breathing easier.
Water enters the stomach and intestines, promoting digestion and absorption, and ensuring smooth bowel movements.

⑤ Water will seep into the gaps in the bones, lubricating the joints and reducing friction in the skeletal joints, making them more flexible.

④ After entering the body for about 60 minutes, water travels to various parts of the body along with the blood.

⑥ Water also travels into the body's cells, delivering nutrients and oxygen to them, then carrying away waste products from the cells, which are filtered by the kidneys and excreted as urine.

Stories Flowing by the Riverbank

People can't live without water, so they gathered by the river. Together, they built houses, hunted prey, found ways to live, fumbled how to make clothes, and even learned to irrigate the land to grow food.

The Four Ancient Civilizations Born along the River

Approximately 5,000 to 6,500 years ago, four ancient civilizations emerged along the great rivers around the world.

Ancient Egypt along the Nile River

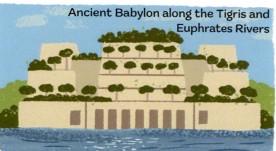

Ancient Babylon along the Tigris and Euphrates Rivers

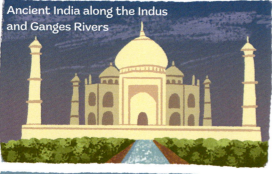

Ancient India along the Indus and Ganges Rivers

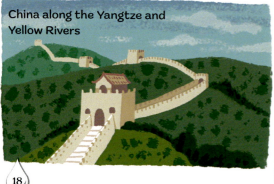

China along the Yangtze and Yellow Rivers

When the River Gets Angry

I lived along the Yangtze River and Yellow River for a long time, watching as the number of people by the riverside grew. The did many interesting things with the river water. Even when the river water sometimes turned into a temperamental "monster," they still sought ways to befriend it.

People used waterwheels to irrigate the fields.

People learned how to drill a well, so they co use water without having to go to the rivers

By using water mills, their work became more efficient.

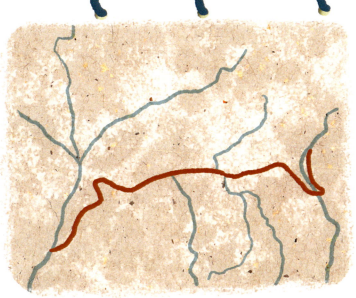

The Lingqu Canal—a Gem of Ancient Water Conservancy Architecture

In the early fifth century BC, the Chinese carved out a grand canal that connected various regions across the land. To manage the sometimes turbulent, sometimes drained river waters, people built many remarkable water conservancy projects.

The construction of the Lingqu Canal showcased the ingenuity of people at that time in dealing with river waters. It not only served transportation and irrigation functions but also included three essential inventions.

Invention no. 1

Water flow could be cut off by using a dam shaped like the Chinese character "人" (human). During the rainy season, it could divert the water to prevent floods. In the dry season, it could alter the river's flow and direct it into other channels.

Invention no. 2

The clever use of cast iron to connect the stones on the dam made it so large and stable that it could still work perfectly after thousands of years.

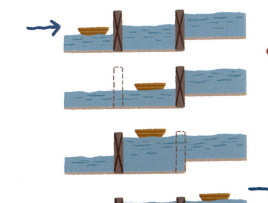

Invention no. 3

Locks were invented to help the ships use buoyancy to rise and fall vertically from a low-water channel into a high-water channel, allowing navigation at different levels.

The Ingenious Chinese

Chinese have many other ingenious inventions.

Various Ways of Crossing Rivers

Cut down a tree to make a single-log bridge.

Stack stones to make small stone bridges.

Zipline over a turbulent river.

The Four Great Inventions of China

Papermaking

Around the second century BC
The Chinese discovered that the fibers of plants could not only make clothes but also thin and light paper. A person named Cai Lun improved the papermaking technique. People who used to write and draw on rock walls, clay tablets, animal bones, and bamboo slips now had a new choice.

Compass

Around the fourth century BC
While mining ores, the Chinese discovered a type of stone with magnetic properties and used these stones to make a directional tool called the south-pointer. This is how the world's earliest compass was born.

Stirrups for Easy Riding

Around AD the third century
As early as 7,000 years ago, humans began to learn to ride horses, but they could only sit on the back of the horse and support the body with the hip to maintain balance. Once the horse galloped, people would easily fall off. However, since the invention of the stirrup in China, riders have been able to use their left and right feet as support points, allowing them to run across the land on horseback and reach farther places.

Singing Chime Bells

Around the sixth century BC
Chinese people have been very fond of music since a long time ago. They created many instruments that produced beautiful sounds using silk threads, bamboo, wood, animal bones, or hides. Chime bells are among the earliest metal percussion instruments in the world, and they are also Chinese people's perfect combination of smelting technology and acoustic knowledge—a true masterpiece of artistry.

Gunpowder

Around AD the seventh century
Some Chinese people who sought immortality became obsessed with alchemy. They put strange things into the furnace again and again, and accidentally produced explosive gunpowder. This unexpected discovery of gunpowder significantly advanced human civilization.

Printing

Around AD the seventh century
The Chinese invented block printing by carving raised characters in reverse on a board, brushing it with ink, and gently pressing it flat on a sheet of paper. Creating a book no longer required the time-consuming and laborious task of hand-copying. Printing allowed the mass production of books, and human wisdom began to spread more easily.

Water Drop's New Game

I also played many interesting games with Chinese people. They brewed tree leaves in water, giving birth to fragrant tea; they moistened clay with water and put it into a hot furnace, creating beautiful and useful ceramics; and they soaked silkworm cocoons in water, producing transparent and delicate silk, just like the wings of the dragonfly. Chinese loved these things, and soon, people all over the world fell in love with them, too.

The Legend of Tea

According to the legend, the earliest discoverer of tea was the Chinese agricultural pioneer Shennong. In his search for food and medicinal herbs, he tasted hundreds of plants and accidentally discovered tea leaves, which quenched his thirst and refreshed his spirit.

Tea leaves became popular across China. Some people dried them before brewing, some people crushed them with various foods and boiled them all together, while others enjoyed grinding the leaves into powder, creating foam, and writing or drawing on top.

The different processing methods gave tea leaves various appearances. Still, Chinese people classified them into six main categories: green tea, white tea, oolong tea, black tea, dark tea, and yellow tea.

In the Tang Dynasty (AD 618–907), a man named Lu Yu wrote *The Classic of Tea*, in which he described everything about tea in detail. Later, people regarded *The Classic of Tea* as the encyclopedia of tea and honored Lu Yu as "the saint of tea."

The Story of Porcelain

As early as 10,000 years ago, people learned to fire pottery from dried clay. But pottery at that time was bulky, not strong or durable, and it was particularly easy to absorb water, leaving food residue. The Chinese began to improve the technique of firing clay and made beautiful and durable porcelain.

The Secret Techniques of Firing Porcelain

Secret technique no. 1
Select kaolin clay as the raw material.

Secret technique no. 2
Fire in a porcelain kiln at temperatures above 1,200°C.

Secret technique no. 3
Coat ceramics with a glassy, transparent glaze while firing.

The Secret of Silk

About 5,000 years ago Chinese people began raising silkworms to make silk and developed an exclusive secret technique. In ancient times, many foreign lords were willing to trade several bags of gold just to get their hands on silk. During the Qin (221–206 BC) and Han (206 BC–AD 220) dynasties, the technique for weaving silk improved, and the demand for silk grew. People even opened up the "Silk Road," a route from China to the Western regions, where they traded silk on camelback.

How Is Silk Made?

Reeling
Boil the cocoons in hot water and reel out raw silk from the top.

Weaving
Weave the silk threads according to the requirements to create silk fabric.

Dyeing
Dye or print silk fabrics with nice patterns.

Along the Sea to Afar

To exchange more interesting items and explore the unknown corners of the world, more and more people sail across the vast oceans guided by the compass. Sometimes I turn into small waves on the sea, watch the busy ships come and go, or push the ships toward places I have never been before . . .

Remarkable Explorers

Marco Polo

Born in Venice, Marco Polo chronicled his travels across the East. Through *The Travels of Marco Polo*, Europeans discovered the mystery and beauty of the ancient countries of the East, and all wanted to set out to see the other side of the world.

Zheng He

Not only did Western explorers sail the seas, but in 1405, the Ming Emperor of China sent Zheng He to establish new maritime routes in the Indian Ocean, bringing the development of the "Maritime Silk Road" to its peak. Zheng He made seven expeditions on the sea, during which he developed many new navigational technologies and showcased China's strength to neighboring countries.

Gradually Evolving Boats

Raft
Wood floating on water led people to discover a method of floating on water. By connecting these logs together they made rafts, the earliest type of boat.

Dugout canoe
Later, people came up with the idea of finding a large tree trunk and hollowing it out. Thus, the dugout canoe, capable of carrying people and cargo, was born.

Scull
Paddles were invented to make boats move faster across the water. However, rowing with paddles was not only laborious, but it also made the boat wobble. In the first century BC, Chinese people invented the scull, which acts like a fish's tail to give the boat a steady push, making rowing more efficient.

Vasco da Gama

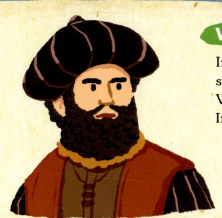

In 1497-1498, influenced deeply by his seafaring father, the Portuguese explorer Vasco da Gama followed the winds of the Indian Ocean to find a route to India.

Columbus

Funded by the Spanish queen, Christopher Columbus set sail westward in 1492 in search of a route to the Indian Ocean. However, he did not discover Asia; instead, he accidentally found a new continent named the Americas.

Magellan

When Europeans became fascinated with the taste of Oriental spices, groups of explorers began to travel the sea in search of spices. In 1519, Ferdinand Magellan from Portugal joined the fleet searching for spices. They rode the waves and found their way to the Pacific Ocean in South America. After a three-year journey, Magellan's fleet completed humankind's first trip around the world, proving that the Earth is indeed a round sphere.

Rudder

How to change the direction of a boat in the water efficiently and safely? For thousands of years, this question puzzled countless navigators. In AD the first century, the Chinese invented the rudder, which uses the power of the water itself to change the direction of the vessel.

Sailboats

In order to make the ship travel faster on the sea, people put sails on the ship and harness the power of the wind to propel the ship further.

The invention of the sailboat makes sea exploration no longer difficult and lengthy.

World-Changing Machines

The power of wind, water, and animals gradually became insufficient to meet people's needs.

Humans sought a more powerful force to assist them, and this time they discovered the power of steam.

Mid-eighteenth Century to Mid-nineteenth Century
The First Industrial Revolution Ushers in the Age of Steam

People conducted in-depth studies on the power of steam. Based on previous research, British engineer James Watt developed a highly efficient new type of steam engine and also created a unit called "horsepower" to measure the energy produced by steam engines. Horsepower is equivalent to the work done by a strong horse; it roughly represents the work done to lift a 75-kilogram object one meter high in one second.

Steam engine did not only help people produce more products in a shorter time, but also bring out the steam locomotive as a new type of transportation. After people changing the wooden rails for the horse-drawn carriages into steal ones, the steam locomotive, billowing the long trails of smoke and rumbling with "whoo-whoo" sounds, raced across the land. Steam engine quickly shortened the distance between the cities and countryside, completely changing people's way of living.

Late-Nineteenth Century to Early-Twentieth Century
The Second Industrial Revolution Ushers in the Age of Electricity

While the power of steam amazed people, the power of electricity and magnetism fascinated them even more. Over 2,500 years ago, ancient Greeks discovered that rubbing amber could produce static electricity that attracted small objects. By 1821, electric motors, which transformed electricity into mechanical motion, and ammeters, which allowed people to see the movement of electrical charges, were created.

In 1871, the Italian man Antonio Meucci invented the earliest telephone to help care for his crippled wife.

In 1879, the news said that an American man named Thomas Edison conducted thousands of experiments and invented the electric light that illuminated the night.

In 1886, the German man Karl Benz created the earliest automobile to save his nearly bankrupt company.

In 1888, I heard that the French man Louis Le Prince had created a movie that allowed people to see dreamlike moving images.

Mid-twentieth Century to Early-Twenty-First Century
The Third Industrial Revolution Ushers in the Age of Information

As we were about to bid farewell to the nineteenth century, scientists discovered particles smaller than atoms, which they named electrons. They began exploring how to incorporate these particles into new inventions.

In 1938, experiments involving electron bombardment revealed the secrets of the atomic nucleus and led scientists to seek ways to utilize nuclear energy.

In 1946, the first computer capable of processing multiple types of information was born.

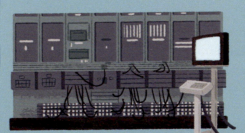

In 1957, the world's first artificial satellite was successfully launched, and humankind began to explore the secrets of space.

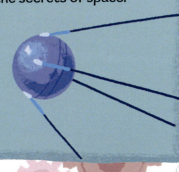

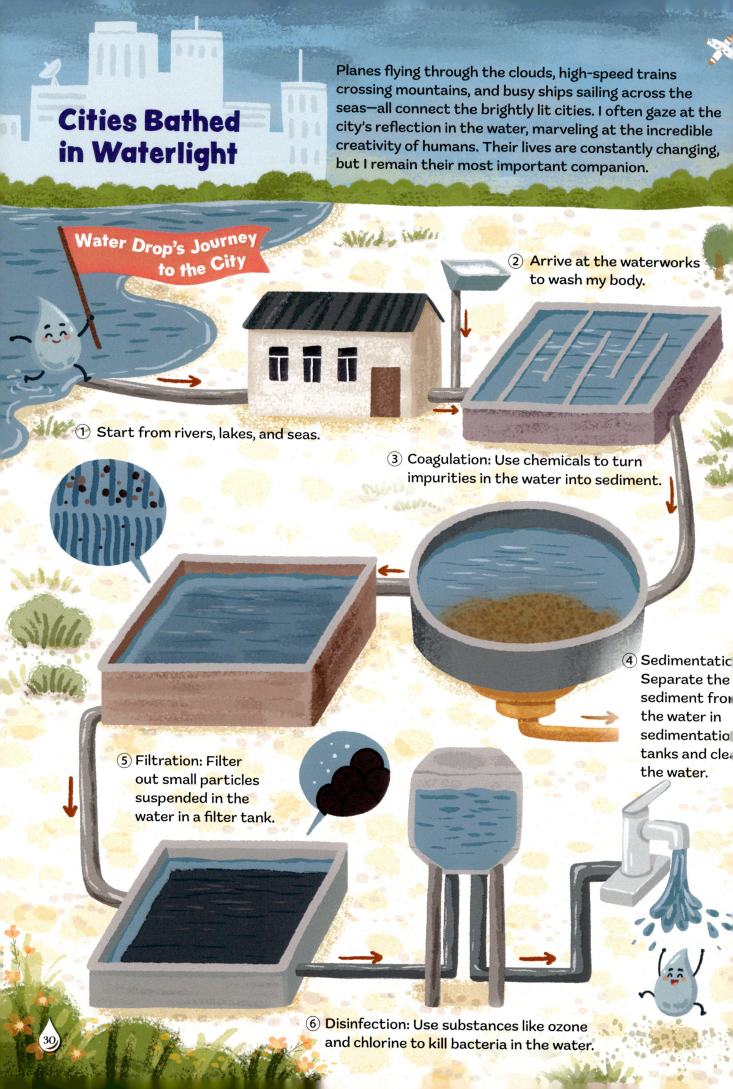

Through water pipes to the water tanks and water towers.

⑧ Poke my head out of the faucet.

⑨ Sewers: Sewers collect the wastewater generated by people's daily lives and rainwater that suddenly falls from the sky, then carry them away from the city. Sewers keep the city clean and prevent the city from being flooded.

⑩ Hydroelectric power plant: Hydroelectric power plants generate electricity for the city by using the power of water flow to drive generators. They also help prevent floods and guide river flows.

People have also mastered the technology of generating electricity using nuclear energy, but the immense power of nuclear energy often comes with terrible dangers.

Scary and Dangerous Things

Human inventions are changing the world, changing the Earth, and also changing every little drop of water like me. Meanwhile, some terrible and dangerous things are slowly happening …

The Earth Having a Fever

In recent years, people have been emitting more dangerous gases into the atmosphere, with over 30 billion tons of carbon dioxide being released annually. This makes the Earth hotter, causing it to suffer from a condition called the "greenhouse effect." Some areas have become extremely dry, while others experience constant rain leading to floods. The surging hot waves in the ocean force sea creatures to move their homes constantly, killing many lives.

Beware of El Niño and La Niña

In the distant oceans, a pair of very powerful "siblings" often appear.

El Niño is the elder bother with the magic power to warm the sea and produce more water vapor.

These vapors float in the air, causing heavy rain and even floods.

La Niña is the little sister with the magic power to cool the sea. When the seawater gets colder, less vapor is flying into the air. Then, there is less rain, and some places may become dry.

The "siblings" often appear alternately, affecting the temperature of the ocean and the weather on Earth. Therefore, scientists are very concerned about their every move. This affects whether crops on Earth will grow tall, whether people in some places will have enough water to drink, whether houses will be flooded in the summer, and whether people will suffer from the cold in the winter …

Sick Ocean Water

People are also discharging more and more household waste and industrial wastewater into the ocean. The sea has contracted a strange disease, becoming acidic and black. The garbage floating in the sea is mistakenly eaten by sea animals, and microplastics can now be found in the bodies of animals even in the North and South Poles. The nuclear wastewater flowing into the ocean is frightening all the animals.

Acidic Rainwater

The polluted sky and ocean water form acid rain falling from the sky. This rainwater corrodes the buildings in cities and harms plants, animals, as well as the land they rely on for survival.

Melting Glaciers

The increasingly hot weather is melting glaciers on Earth continually. The sea level gets higher every year, while the land shrinks. Ancient bacteria that were once frozen in glaciers may also awaken, bringing terrifying diseases.

Saving a Water Drop

We are sick, we need help!

What types of water are there on Earth?

Seawater, lake water, river water, groundwater, atmospheric water, biological water …

The ocean holds more than 97% of the Earth's water, while usable freshwater is very scarce. Most of the freshwater is frozen in the Arctic, Antarctic, and high up in the snowy mountains.

A Press Conference of "Save a Drop of Water"

Factories need to treat wastewater discharges more seriously and invent more efficient equipment to reduce pollution and waste of water.

When cultivating land, use organic fertilizers to avoid harming the land and water sources with pesticides and chemical fertilizers.

We should always test the water quality to treat it promptly while also protecting the oceans and water sources to prevent water pollution from worsening.

Only by saving water can we save the planet!

Everyone can join the action to save a drop of water. Care for water, save the water.

Protecting Water in Action

Do not throw garbage into rivers or the sea.

Do not recklessly discard harmful pollutants such as used batteries and expired medicines.

Reduce the use of plastic bags and tableware.

Avoid using detergents that pollute the environment when washing clothes and bathing.

Cherish Every Water Drop

Water used for rinsing rice or cooking noodles has good oil-removing ability and can be used to wash dishes.

Water from washing vegetables or keeping fish can promote plant growth and can be used to water flowers.

Bathwater and laundry water can be collected to flush toilets.

Turn off the faucet when brushing your teeth and washing your face, avoiding wasting any single droplet of water.

Do Not Waste Any Food

Every bit of food production, like bread and milk, requires a lot of water. So by not wasting food, you are also saving water.

The Wonderous Journey of a Water Drop

Written by Wang Rong
Illustrated by Ren Jia and Zheng Hui
Translated by Sun Qingyue

First published in 2025 by Royal Collins Publishing Group Inc.
Groupe Publication Royal Collins Inc.
550-555 boul. René-Lévesque O Montréal (Québec) H2Z1B1 Canada

Original edition © Hohai University Press

All rights reserved. Without limiting the rights under copyright reserved above, no part of this publication may be reproduced, stored in or introduced into a retrieval system, or transmitted in any form or by any means (electronic, mechanical, photocopying, recording, or otherwise), without the prior written permission of both the copyright owner and the above publisher of this book.

ISBN: 978-1-4878-1302-4

To find out more about our publications,
please visit www.royalcollins.com.